My First Book About Turtles

I0422874

Amazing Animal Books
Children's Picture Books

By Molly Davidson

Mendon Cottage Books

JD-Biz Publishing

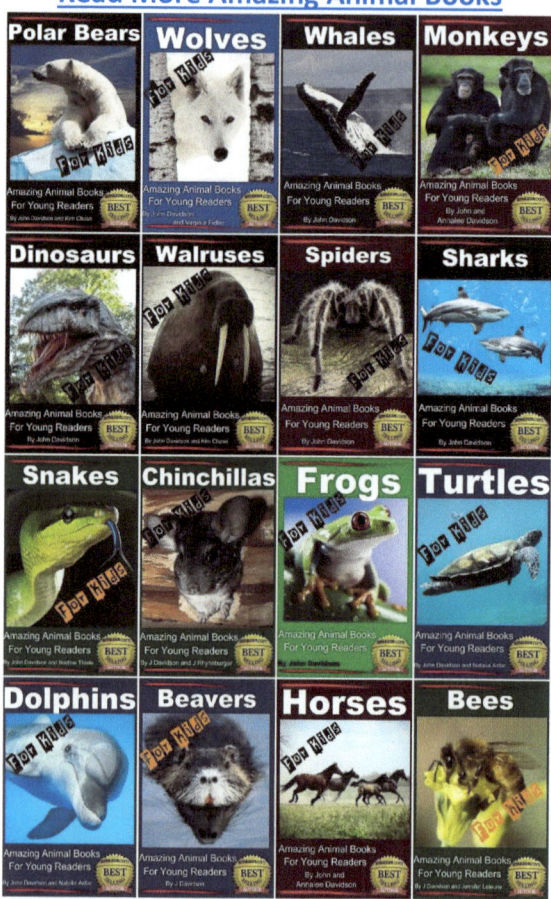

Table of Contents

Introduction 4

Turtles Parts 6

Turtle Defense..8

Turtles As Pets 9

Turtle Care...11

What does a Tortoise eat? 12

Turtle Habitat 13

Types of Turtles 14

Desert Tortoise 17

Sea Tortoise..18

Giant Tortoise..19

Green Turtles...21

Box Turtle 22

Loggerhead Turtle...23

Interesting Facts about the Tortoise.......................25

Turtle Facts..27

Publisher...34

Introduction

Turtles are a reptile.

Its body is protected by a bony shell.

There are two main groups of turtles:

1. Sea Turtle: This kind of turtle is big in size and are found in the Ocean.

2. Fresh Water Turtle: This turtle also called a tortoise and lives on the land. They are smaller than the Sea turtles.

The size of turtles can be from an inch to 6 feet!

Turtles can live for a long time, more than a 150 years.

Turtles have lived since the time of dinosaurs, almost 200 million years ago.

Turtles Parts

Head: All the turtles have a head covered by hard scales.

Mouth: Turtles do not have any teeth! They have horny ridges for cutting food and very strong jaws which they use for capturing and tearing their prey.

Legs and Feet: Tortoises have short legs and feet. Sea turtles legs are used as flippers, this makes them very fast swimmers.

The Shell: The shell which covers the top part of a turtle's body is called "Carapace".

Some turtles do not have a shell; they have a soft shell made of thick skin.

The shell protects the turtles' insides, they cannot take it off.

Tail: All kinds of turtle have tails; it is usually hidden inside the shell.

Turtle Defense

A turtle spends lots of time on land, its shell protects it from predators.

If a turtle feels afraid it will pull its head, legs, and tail inside its shell.

Some turtles defend themselves with a bad smelling yellow fluid which is called musk.

Other turtles will bite and claw their enemies.

Turtles As Pets

If you want to have a turtle as your pet, first you need to ask your parents for permission.

The next step is to choose which type of turtle would be best for you.

Next you need to find out how to keep your turtle happy and healthy.

Set up a place for your turtle, make sure to include water, this is where they will spend lots of their time.

Now, have fun with your pet turtle.

Turtle Care

Giving the turtle enough room to live in, making sure it has enough light, shade and moisture, and clean water.

Your turtle needs shelter so when it is tired it can hide. This can be wood or stones.

Be sure to wash your hands before and after playing with your turtle, they are an animal, not a toy.

What does a Tortoise eat?

They should be eating the plants and weeds growing in your garden, grass, and leaves as well.

You should not feed your turtle strawberries, blueberries, papaya, or raspberries. This is may create many health problems for your tortoise.

Turtle Habitat

An outside pond is the best habitat for your turtle, but if you do not have one of those, a glass aquarium is the next best thing.

An inside aquarium can be cleaned easily.

You can also add live or plastic plants to your turtles' aquarium.

Make sure live plants are not poisonous to turtles, because they will try to eat them.

Types of Turtles

There are more than 300 different types of turtles found all over the earth.

Peninsula Cotter Turtle: It is an easy free pet that needs very little attention. As long as these turtles have a watery place and somewhere to hang out in the sun, they are happy.

Green Sea turtle: It is a quick learner and very playful. People love them as pets.

Saw Back Turtle: Another great pet turtle, they are also known as the "map turtle." The turtle has cream, green, and yellow on its body, which make it look like a road map.

Australian Pig Nosed Turtle: This kind of turtles really loves fresh water. If you put them in an aquarium, do not put other reptiles or big fish, they scare the turtle, so do birds.

Desert Tortoise

Desert Tortoises' grow to be about 9 - 15 inches long.

Tortoises can live up to 80 years!

These tortoises like to eat grasses, bushes, cactus, and their flowers.

Sea Tortoise

Sea tortoises are cold blooded.

Many of them like to live in the tropical warm waters.

 Other sea turtles like the places where water is cooler.

Sea turtles cannot pull their head and legs inside their shells.

They spend most of their time under water.

Giant Tortoise

The giant tortoise is the world's largest tortoise.

Each one can weigh up to 900 pounds!

These tortoises need lot of ground to feed on; they usually live on tropical islands.

Having a giant tortoise as a pet is not a good idea, it's too big, needs lots of space, and cannot be kept indoors.

They eat grasses, leaves, fruit, and lots of cactus.

Giant Tortoises are becoming extinct; the zoo is about the only place you can find them.

Green Turtles

The green turtle is a kind of sea turtle; they can have a green or black shell.

They are the only sea turtles that just eat plants.

Like most sea turtles, green turtles have to swim a long distance so they can lay their eggs.

Box Turtle

Box turtles get their name because their shell looks like a box on their back.

These turtles are from North America and they live mostly on land.

If you would like a box turtle as a pet, they will need to be kept outside.

Loggerhead Turtle

Loggerhead is a type of sea turtle that is found all over the World.

Loggerhead Turtles grow to be between 3 - 9 feet long.

They can weigh as much as 300 pounds.

These turtles have strong jaws; they use these to fight off predators.

They eat mainly worms, star fish, and sea insects.

These turtles are very slow on land, but luckily they spend most of their time in salt water, where they are fast swimmers.

Interesting Facts about the Tortoise

Tortoises are one of the oldest creatures still living on the earth.

There are 60 different bones that make the tortoise's shell.

The desert tortoise can survive ground temperatures as hot as 140°F.

Adult tortoises can survive many years without water

Tortoises don't have flippers but turtles do.

Mother tortoises will lay up to 12 eggs in a deep hole in the sand.

The eggs take 3 - 4 months to hatch.

Turtle Facts

Green turtles can run 20 miles per hour (mph) on land, if they feel attacked.

Turtles can see an extra color which humans cannot see.

Scientists call a turtle's shell a "dust bag".

Some sea turtles can swim as fast as 35 mph!

Baby turtles are called "sparkies."

Read More Amazing Animal Books

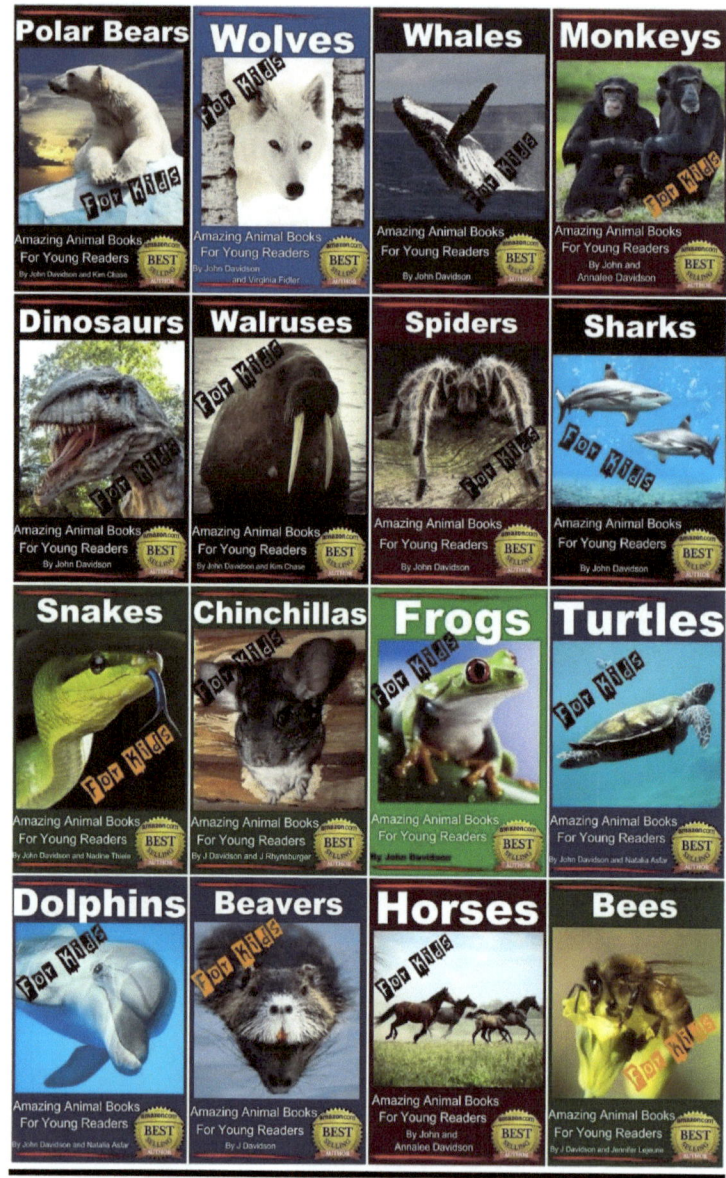

Purchase at Amazon.com
Website http://AmazingAnimalBooks.com

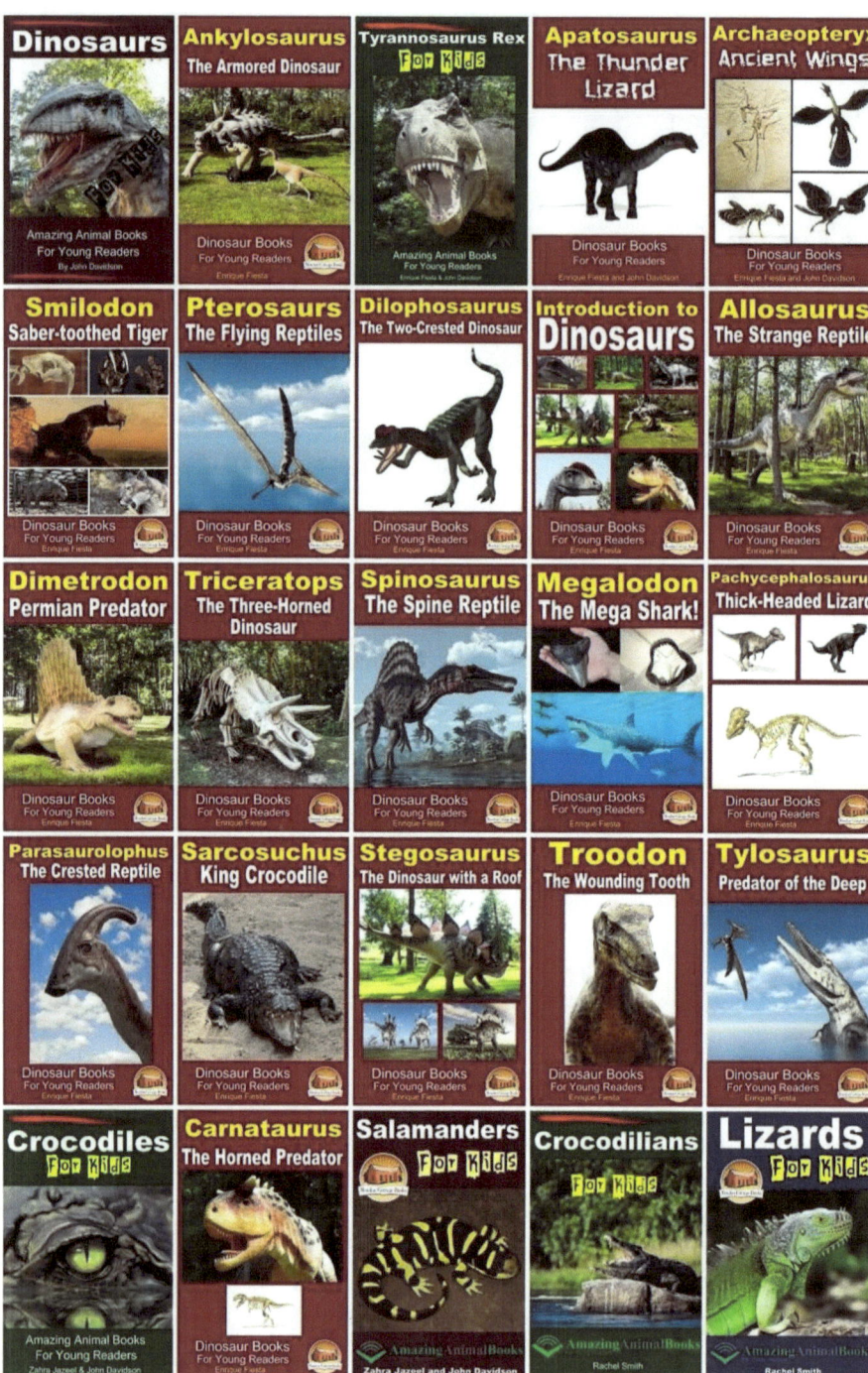

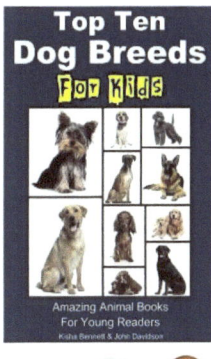
Top Ten Dog Breeds For Kids
Amazing Animal Books For Young Readers
Kisha Bennett & John Davidson

German Shepherds
Dog Books for Kids
K. Bennett

Bulldogs
Dog Books for Kids
K. Bennett

Dachshund
Dog Books for Kids
K. Bennett

Poodles
Dog Books for Kids
K. Bennett

Labrador Retrievers
Dog Books for Kids
K. Bennett

Rottweilers
Dog Books for Kids
K. Bennett

Boxers
Dog Books for Kids
K. Bennett

Golden Retrievers
Dog Books for Kids
K. Bennett

Puppies
Dog Books For Kids
Amazing Animal Books
By John Davidson

Beagles
Dog Books for Kids
K. Bennett

Yorkshire Terriers
Dog Books for Kids
K. Bennett

Dogs Top Ten Dog Breeds For Kids
Amazing Animal Books For Young Readers
Zahra Jazeer & John Davidson

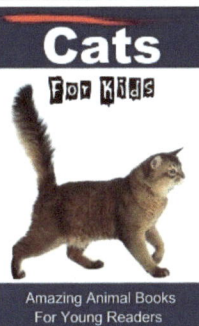
Cats For Kids
Amazing Animal Books For Young Readers
K. Bennett & John Davidson

Foxes For Kids
Amazing Animal Books For Young Readers
Zahra Jazeel & John Davidson

Wolves For Kids
Amazing Animal Books For Young Readers
By John Davidson and Virginia Fidler

Our books are available at

1. Amazon.com

2. Barnes and Noble

3. Itunes

4. Kobo

5. Smashwords

6. Google Play Books

Download Free Books!
http://MendonCottageBooks.com

Publisher

JD-Biz Corp

P O Box 374

Mendon, Utah 84325

http://www.jd-biz.com/